LET'S GO TEAM:
Cheer, Dance, March

LET'S GO TEAM:
Cheer, Dance, March

Competitive CHEERLEADING

Craig Peters

Mason Crest Publishers
Philadelphia

To Alexandra: Keep smiling, maintain your self-confidence, stay focused, and never give up . . . especially when the competition judges aren't watching.

Mason Crest Publishers, Inc.
370 Reed Road
Broomall, PA 19008
(866) MCP-BOOK (toll free)
www.masoncrest.com

2 3 4 5 6 7 8 9 10

Library of Congress Cataloging-in-Publication Data

Peters, Craig, 1958-
  Competitive cheerleading / Craig Peters.
      v. cm. — (Let's go team—cheer, dance, march)
  Includes index.
  Contents: The thrill of competition — A brief history of cheerleading
— Spirit or sport? — Inside the team — The competitive landscape.
   ISBN 1-59084-532-3
   1. Cheerleading—Juvenile literature. [1.
Cheerleading—Competitions.] I. Title. II. Series.
   LB3635 .P435 2003
   791.6'4—dc21

                                                                 2002015953

Produced by
Choptank Syndicate and Chestnut Productions
226 South Washington Street
Easton, Maryland 21601

Project Editors Norman Macht and Mary Hull
Design Lisa Hochstein
Picture Research Mary Hull

Printed and bound in the Hashemite Kingdom of Jordan

OPPOSITE TITLE PAGE
To compete successfully, a cheerleading squad must be focused, spirited, and athletic. The squad needs to synchronize its movements and make the transitions from stunt to stunt smoothly.

Table of Contents

The Thrill of Competition

The excitement is like nothing you've ever experienced. There's electricity in the air. Your senses are on high alert. It's the kind of atmosphere you imagine it must be like backstage at a major concert event or Hollywood awards show.

You're standing in the hallway of a large high school, surrounded by your teammates. Your moment in the spotlight is just minutes away. Your coach is waiting for the call to bring your team into the gymnasium. You hear the thumping bass of the music in the gym, a rumbling accompaniment to the voices of another competition squad, rising in unison as the cheerleaders make their way

A team member held aloft by other cheerleaders is called a flyer. Cheerleaders who lift and provide support for flyers are called bases.

through the routine they have practiced hundreds of times.

Practice. You've certainly had plenty of that. Two hours a night, three nights a week, plus extra practices on the weekends, for almost three months. Gymnastics classes and dance classes have helped, too.

For a moment, you start to worry. If you're a base, one of the team members whose job is to lift other cheerleaders and provide support for pyramids, you may recall a time when the flyer came down at a slightly wrong angle. Her head grazed your chin. Nothing serious happened, but it could have been a lot worse. You may have heard stories about incidents when a base who wasn't paying proper attention had some teeth knocked out by a flyer. You hope nothing like that happens today. Not today, not in front of the judges, the other squads, the standing-room-only crowd of parents and friends, and your teammates.

The worry passes in an instant as you see another squad passing yours. They're talking animatedly about having competed only minutes earlier. You hear bits and pieces of conversation; words and phrases like "judges" and "the audience" and "scoring sheet" and "cartwheels" swarm in your ears. It's impossible to make sense of it all, so you don't even try. You have to focus on your own competition routine.

It's hard to focus, though, because so much activity is going on all around you, and part of you can't even believe you're here. You had hoped that you would make the team. There was the pre-tryout meeting, at which you

When performing in competitions, it is especially important to smile, project your voice, keep your head up, and make eye contact with the judges.

learned a few cheers and routines. On top of those, you added a few basic jumps and stunts of your own. You practiced every night at home. Then there were the try-outs themselves. After making the first cut, you practiced every night for the next round of tests. You did your warm-ups, dressed correctly, stuck to your routines, and tried not to be nervous.

Once you made the team, it was only the beginning. You had to learn the competition routine while getting to know and trust your teammates. They, in turn, needed to get to know and trust you.

As you wait to go on, you remind yourself to make eye contact with the judges. Keep your head up, and don't forget to smile. It's so easy to not smile when you're concentrating on the routine, but you also don't want to grin like some kind of bizarre Barbie doll. You want to be loud and project your voice into the crowd, but you don't want to shriek or scream.

You can hear the crowd noise filtering through the halls of the school. It sounds like a hundred thousand frenzied sports fans screaming for their team during a close championship game in the bottom of the ninth inning or the last minutes of the fourth quarter. You imagine what it must be like inside the gym. It seems like

COMPETITION TIPS

- Prepare a checklist of everything the squad will need to take to the competition and check each item off the list as it is packed.

- When you arrive at the place of competition, familiarize yourselves with the facilities.

- Confirm the competition schedule and make sure all squad members know where they need to be and when.

- Be friendly and supportive of the other squads.

- Assign someone to take notes or pictures during your performance; you can go over the notes later and use them to help improve your next performance.

- Don't forget to have fun!

the Super Bowl and the World Series and the NBA finals all rolled into one, and everyone's going to be looking directly at you.

The music inside the gym changes. It's not competition music anymore; it's the music that's played while one team leaves the floor and the next team enters.

"All right, everyone, let's go!"

Your coach's words seem unreal. You've played this moment over and over in your mind a hundred times or more. Here you are, though, and it's nothing like you imagined it would be. It's exciting, exhilarating, and invigorating. It's better than you ever hoped.

The cheers of the crowd are almost drowned out by the stamping of their feet on the bleachers. Your head seems to be swimming in the noise as your team runs into the center of the gym and takes their position on the mat. The sound begins to die down as everyone realizes that your team is about to begin its routine.

You hold your position. You make eye contact with the judge at the table right in front of you. You smile and are motionless as you await your cue. Then the voice comes over the sound system saying the words you've heard so many times as an audience member. They're words that signal the start of not just your first competition, but of a life-shaping journey down the exciting and challenging road of competitive cheerleading. They're the equivalent of "hike" at the Super Bowl or "play ball" at the World Series, and only later will you start to understand how they have meaning far beyond this particular moment.

"You may begin."

A Brief History of Cheerleading

As college football's popularity grew in the first half of the twentieth century, cheerleading's popularity grew along with it. By the 1920s, gymnastics had become incorporated into cheerleading routines. Women were generally lighter, and easier to lift, so women became more active in cheerleading.

Paper pom pons (sometimes the hyphenated version, "pom-pons," is used, but the often-seen "pom-poms" is actually incorrect) were introduced to cheerleading in the 1930s. The origin of the word pom pon is unclear. However, it may be derived from the french word "pompe" meaning "display" or "parade." There are also

Cheerleaders began using pom pons in the 1930s, although at that time they were made of paper. Vinyl pom pons were not introduced until the 1960s.

Cheerleading grew in popularity during the 1950s, and cheerleaders began wearing a uniform: a letter sweater and a skirt with a hemline below the knee.

canine grooming references: a "tail pom" is when the tip of a dog's tail is groomed into a fluffy ball, and the rest of the tail is like a stick

Cheerleading became a mostly female activity in the 1940s when many young men were in the armed forces during World War II. When the war ended and men returned from the battlefields to the playing fields, cheerleading saw a growth in the popularity of partner stunts and gymnastics.

In 1948, Lawrence R. Herkimer started the National Cheerleaders Association in his hometown of Dallas, Texas. In 1949, he organized the first camp for cheerleaders at Sam Houston State University in Huntsville, Texas.

According to the National Cheerleaders Association (NCA):

Fifty-two girls attended the seminar, which also included a speech professor to present tips on speaking in front of an audience, and an English teacher to aid with cheer rhymes, Neither the English teacher nor the speech teacher impressed the 52 girls, but Herkie did. He used gymnastics

CELEBRITY CHEERLEADERS

Cheerleading is an activity that helps focus one's attention toward personal excellence and growth. So it comes as no surprise that many celebrities were once cheerleaders. Here's a small list of some of the best-known (and perhaps most surprising) examples:

Actors: Kirk Douglas, Samuel L. Jackson, Jack Lemmon, Steve Martin, Luke Perry, James Stewart

Actresses: Halle Berry, Sandra Bullock, Cameron Diaz, Kirsten Dunst, Calista Flockhart, Terri Hatcher, Kelly Ripa, Sela Ward, Reese Witherspoon

Musicians: Paula Abdul, Christina Aguilera, Toni Basil, Faith Hill, Lauryn Hill, Madonna, "Dixie Chick" Natalie Maines, Reba McEntire

Presidents: George W. Bush, Dwight D. Eisenhower, Ronald Reagan, Franklin D. Roosevelt

As cheerleading continues to become more gymnastic in nature, strict safety standards and guidelines are even more important to insure that difficult moves are always performed in the safest possible way.

and vigorous motions to show them how to stimulate and direct crowd response. The girls were elated. They had experienced a totally innovative phenomenon.

Through the 1950s, cheerleading reached new heights of popularity. "Girls really took over for the first time," wrote Kieran Scott in *Ultimate Cheerleading.*

It was a nice, pure, all-American thing for the teenage girl to do to support her male peers as they sweated it out on the field and on the court. Cheerleaders were often elected by the student body, not unlike homecoming or prom

A TURNING POINT IN CHEERLEADING HISTORY?

On August 22, 2000, the comedy *Bring It On* made its premiere in the United States where cheerleading was growing in popularity among junior high and high school-aged girls. The movie, starring Kirsten Dunst, tells the story of two rival high school cheerleading squads who are competing for a coveted national championship. One of the squads learns that their best cheering routines were stolen from the rival team by their former captain.

The summer movie was a hit. It ranked number one the first weekend it appeared in theaters. There probably isn't a cheerleader in her teens who hasn't seen the movie a dozen or more times.

Bring It On gave the athletic discipline of competitive cheerleading an enormous boost in popularity. Millions of parents who weren't aware of the existence of competitive cheerleading before *Bring It On* certainly found out about it as a result of the movie. Many of those parents saw their children sign up for cheerleading classes and squads as the 2000 back to school season got underway.

In the movie, Kirsten Dunst's character, Torrance Shipman, asks Eliza Dushku's character, Missy Pantone, "Ever been to a cheerleading competition?" Pantone replies, "What do you mean, like a football game?" to which Shipman says, "No, not a football game, those are like practices for us."

With that small exchange of dialogue, *Bring It On* explained competitive cheerleading to the largest audience cheerleading has ever had. It also helped to change many of the stereotypes that people have held for years about cheerleaders.

Professional football teams began using cheerleaders to motivate the team and fans as early as the 1950s. The Baltimore Colts were the first major league football team to hire professional cheerleaders.

queens. You didn't really need all that much more than a pretty smile and a sunny disposition to make the squad.

The 1950s saw the creation of the first professional cheerleading squad in National Football League (NFL) history, the Baltimore Colts Cheerleaders.

In the 1960s the vinyl pom pon was invented and the International Cheerleading Foundation (ICF) presented its first annual ranking of the "Top 10 College Cheer Squads." On the grade school and collegiate levels, cheerleading began spreading to all sports, moving beyond the traditional cheering sports of football and basketball.

By the 1970s, cheerleading seemed to be everywhere. The Dallas Cowboy Cheerleaders performed at Super Bowl X in 1976, though their style of cheerleading was strong on smiles, hair, and posing, and weak on athletic skills and choreography.

In 1978 the CBS network broadcast the Collegiate Cheerleading Championships, held by the International Cheerleading Foundation. The broadcast to a nationwide audience helped cheerleading receive recognition as a serious athletic activity. Cheerleading organizations established formal safety guidelines and standards. They outlawed dangerous and potentially crippling moves and pyramids. National competitions were established not just for the collegiate level, but also for grade and high school cheerleaders. The Pop Warner Little Scholars program, a national youth cheerleading, dance, and football organization, hosted its first cheerleading competition in 1988. Pop Warner emphasizes athletics and education. Unless participants make satisfactory progress at school, they are not allowed to compete.

Through the 1990s and into the 21st century, cheerleading has continued to enjoy amazing growth in popularity. There are countless cheering camps and competitions nationwide. In 2000, the inaugural World Cheerleading Championship was held, featuring squads from a dozen countries. *Time* magazine reported in November 2000 that nearly a third of all U.S. colleges had competitive teams, and nearly 200 colleges offered cheerleading scholarships. They also pointed out the growth in male cheerleading, reporting that in 1999 the number

While there have always been male cheerleaders on the college level, the number of male cheerleaders on the high school level has grown dramatically in recent years.

of high school male cheerleaders doubled, to 1,200. *Newsweek* magazine estimated in 2001 that there were approximately 2,500 gyms or clubs nationwide with cheering squads. In 2002, *USA Today* reported that an estimated half-million cheerleaders attended cheering camps each summer.

The increase in interest is strongest in the United States, but similar trends are occurring in Canada, England, Germany, Japan, and elsewhere. In 2002, Canada held its first Canadian National Cheerleading Championships. Cheer Force Wolfpack from Burlington, Ontario, winners of the All-Star Club finals, took the Grand Championship.

With more than 4 million cheerleaders in 50 countries worldwide, the future of cheerleading certainly looks bright.

Spirit or Sport?

Willis Bugbee, author of *Just Yells,* the first book on cheerleading, wrote in 1927:

"The cheerleader, where once merely tolerated, is now a person of regal estate. His prestige is such that in many schools and colleges he must win his place through competitive examinations."

Rick Reilly, a noted writer for *Sports Illustrated,* wrote in 1999:

"Oh, right, nowadays cheerleading is classified as a sport . . . if cheerleading is a sport, Richard Simmons is a ballerina. It's athletic, but it's not a sport. In fact, what's sad is that most cheerleaders would make fine athletes."

Whether performed on the sidelines of a football field or at a national cheer championship, cheerleading is athletically demanding.

It would seem that cheerleading hasn't made a lot of progress in the public eye in 70 years. In fact, Reilly's opinion represents a declining number of people as cheerleading continues to gain more respect. Cheerleaders are finally being recognized as legitimate athletes, not just pep rally participants.

Cheerleaders and cheerleading coaches write letters to school and local newspapers to explain the athletic demands of cheerleading, and people are listening. States are listening, too, but it's not always easy to know exactly which ones are paying attention. According to Susan Loomis, the "spirit rules liaison" for the National Federation of State High School Associations, somewhere between 17 and 20 of the 50 states defined cheerleading as a sport in 2002. "The number is always in flux," she told *USA Today.* "I can't tell you the exact number, and that's my job."

There are two sides to cheerleading: spirit and athleticism. The heated debate over whether cheerleading is a sport or not illustrates the importance of each of those two sides.

On the one hand, cheerleading is about team spirit and positive attitude. That's where cheerleading's roots are. It's a way to support a team that is struggling to win a game, and a way to celebrate a team's accomplishments on the playing field. It's about developing self-confidence and personal excellence, setting goals, and working hard to attain them. It's also about learning to work with other people in a team environment. Even at the highest levels of cheerleading competition, non-athletic concerns take

Cheerleading was originally developed as a way to stir up crowd interest in sports like football and lift the spirits of the school team.

center stage. Cheerleaders and coaches know that if the smiles aren't bright and wide enough, if the eye contact with the judges isn't there and the hair and makeup aren't just right, their team will suffer on the scoring sheet.

On the other hand, cheerleading can be a highly demanding physical activity. Many cheerleaders work as hard, if not harder, than their counterparts on traditional sports teams. There are squad practices, gymnastics classes, individual training sessions, and even the physical injuries associated with traditional sports. The Consumer Product Safety Commission reported an estimated 4,954 hospital emergency room visits in 1980 caused by cheer-leading injuries. By 1986 the number had increased to 6,911, and in 1994 the number increased to approximately 16,000. The most common cheerleading injuries are busted lips and broken arms.

As one popular bumper sticker often seen in the parking lots at cheerleading competitions states, "Cheer-leading: If it were any easier, it would be called football."

It is fair to say that many people confuse the question "Is cheerleading a sport?" with the question "Are cheer-leaders athletes?" Few people would dispute that many cheerleaders are superb athletes. The question of whether cheerleading is a sport or not, though, affects more than a cheerleader's pride. It could also affect the squad's legal status.

In 1972, Congress passed what is known as the Title IX section of the Educational Amendments law. The goal of the law was to prevent discrimination against girls and women in education that is funded by the government. That protection against discrimination extends to a school's sports fields as well as its classrooms.

Under the law, public schools must provide equal opportunities, equipment, funding, and facilities to sports teams of both genders.

So the question of whether cheerleading is a sport or not became that much more complicated. If a state recog-nized cheerleading as a sport, then the cheerleading programs needed to conform to Title IX laws, raising some questions:

- Is selection for the cheerleading team based strictly on objective factors related to athletic ability?
- Is the cheerleading team limited to a defined season?
- Is the cheerleading team administered by the school's athletic department?

THE BEST OF BOTH WORLDS

Is cheerleading a school activity like orchestra and choir or a sanctioned sport like football and basketball?

In many ways cheerleading is both, but once it's defined as a sport, things change. Sports have to pay attention to rules and regulations that activities don't have to worry about. So for many coaches and squads, the best of both worlds is to have people respecting cheerleaders as athletes while operating under the definition of cheerleading as an activity.

"The people who run cheerleading are happy to have it as an important activity that is not defined as a sanctioned sport," said Ronnie Carter, president of the National Federation of High School Athletic Associations, in 2002. "In states where it is a sport, teams can't go on to national competitions."

They also can't practice year-round if they're a sanctioned varsity team. That places an official varsity squad at a serious disadvantage against an activity squad, which might practice for 11 months on a specific routine before taking it to a competition.

Sport or no sport, that's not a level playing field.

Cheerleading has evolved into an athletic activity that many consider to be a sport itself. While cheerleaders still support school teams, they are also competitors in regional, national, and world cheerleading competitions.

- Is the primary purpose of the team athletic competition or the support and promotion of other athletes and teams?

In 1995 Title IX wasn't much of an issue anymore where cheerleading was concerned. That's when the U.S. Department of Education's Office for Civil Rights said that cheerleading would not be considered when looking at the question of whether boys and girls are receiving the same opportunities.

Title IX issues aside, the question of whether cheerleading is a sport or not means a lot. It also affects a lot more than just the pride of the cheerleaders themselves. It could affect a team's funding, and it definitely affects the rules under which they operate.

The Women's Sports Foundation (WSF) made a public statement on the issue in July 2000. In it, the WSF attempted to address the question of what defines something as a sport. "The most commonly accepted definition of a sport activity includes all of the following elements," the WSF wrote:

- A physical activity which involves propelling a mass through space or overcoming the resistance of a mass.
- A contest or competition against or with an opponent.
- The sport activity is governed by rules which explicitly define the time, space, and purpose of the contest and the conditions under which a winner is declared.
- The acknowledged primary purpose of the competition is a comparison of the relative skills of the participants.

After seeing this statement, the American Association of Cheerleading Coaches and Advisors (AACCA) agreed with the WSF. They, too, said that because there's no competition against an opponent, cheerleading is not actually a sport. They added, though, that "the long-held view of cheerleading as merely another school activity is also a concern. If the athleticism of cheerleading is not recognized, the supervision will continue to fall to teachers that are not qualified to adequately supervise."

The American Association of Cheerleading Coaches and Advisors went on to suggest that maybe the question of "sport or activity?" shouldn't be asked at all. Maybe a better way to go is to create a new category called "athletic activity." The AACCA wrote:

> Some states are now officially recognizing cheerleaders as "student athletes," which provides opportunities for academic honors and even coverage under the athletic catastrophic insurance policy. State activities and athletic associations are working together with state cheerleading coaches' associations to provide training in safety and the day-to-day program development needed to continue this participation in cheerleading. In this category of "athletic activity," where the participants are recognized as "student athletes," cheerleading can continue to provide great benefits to both the participants and the entire school community.

"Athletic activity" doesn't seem like a bad compromise. Then again, will the idea of participating in an "athletic activity" really satisfy those people who feel that cheerleaders should be recognized on the same level as football or basketball players? It's easy to imagine the put-downs in the school hallway: "You're not part of a sport, you're part of an athletic activity."

Maybe the problem with trying to answer the "activity or sport?" question is simply that it can't be answered. Cheerleading is both. To say that cheerleading needs to be one or the other is like saying that a movie has to be either pictures or sound. It can't be. It is both.

Something that everyone can agree on is that cheer-leading squads can be looked at in much the same ways as athletic teams. In the case of cheerleading teams, as with any kind of team, each member of the team has a specific job to do.

Inside the Team

Not every football player can be a quarterback. There are many different positions on a football team, and those positions should be filled depending on the skills of the individual athletes involved. Someone who's a fast runner and a good catcher will be a solid candidate for a position like wide receiver. Someone else who's larger and more aggressive would be a good candidate to be a defensive lineman.

It is much the same with cheerleading. There are many types of cheerleading squads. Some squads emphasize dance routines, others focus on pom pon routines. Some cheerleading squads perform only on the sidelines during

A cheerleading squad is composed of members with distinct roles. In addition to a coach, each squad has its own bases, flyers, tumblers, and spotters.

school games; others exist solely for the sake of competition. Some do a bit of both.

If you've decided to join a competition cheerleading squad, you've made a decision that will require a lot of hard work and dedication. It also means that you may need to change some of your expectations for the good of the team. You may want to be a flyer, but your coach may feel you're better for the team as a base. For

WHAT ABOUT THE BOYS?

Cheerleading was an all-male activity up to the 1920s. During the '20s, cheerleaders began adding stunts to their routines that involved lifting team members into the air. Because women were generally easier to lift than men, women were welcomed onto cheering squads.

Today, cheerleading is a predominantly female activity, but the participation of males is growing. In June 2001, *American Cheerleader* magazine instituted a new column, "It's A Guy Thing," celebrating this small but growing segment of the cheerleading world.

In its December 2001 issue, *American Cheerleader* reported on the results of an Internet poll they conducted. The number-one reason to have guys on a competition team? "Better stunting!" was the answer given by an overwhelming 80 percent. The other two answers in the poll were "They pump you up!" (11 percent) and "They can work a crowd!" (9 percent).

With better stunting so important in competition cheerleading, it's no wonder *American Cheerleader* calls male cheerleaders "a sought-after commodity come trophy-hunting season."

Male cheerleaders are in demand, in part because their strength can help a squad perform show-stopping stunts.

the good of your team, you will need to respect the coach's opinion.

A strong coach is very important for a competition squad. A coach must be dedicated to helping everyone do their best, building self-confidence in each individual, while considering the needs of the team. There needs to be an understanding of the stresses that competition can bring, and a knowledge of the limits to which that squad can be taken. If the coach pushes the squad too far, it could hurt the members of the squad physically or mentally.

A strong coach must focus each individual's efforts toward the success of the team. Through it all, the members of the squad should be having fun and growing as individuals.

In addition to the coach, there are five main jobs on a competition squad. As you read through the descriptions, think about not just what you would like to do, but about what you are most suited to doing, both physically and mentally.

THE MENTAL FACTOR

Competitive cheering is not just physically demanding, it's mentally demanding, too. As a member of a competition team, you aren't just cheering in front of a crowd, you're being graded by judges. Anytime you try to win something, you're taking a chance you might lose. That means that you have to be mentally strong as well as physically fit to handle the pressures and demands of competition.

Here are some questions to ask yourself to find out if you have what it takes:

Do you feel you can handle yourself well in front of a critical audience? Are your friends and family supportive of your cheerleading efforts? Do you have a coach you can talk to about any problems, worries, or doubts you might have about competitions? Are the fellow members of your squad not just members of a squad, but genuine teammates joined together in a team effort to succeed? Do you feel that doing your best and learning from your mistakes is more important than winning or losing?

If you can answer "yes" to all of those questions, you are well on your way to having a mental attitude that complements your physical capabilities.

Bases need strong arms, shoulders, and legs, as well as excellent balance, in order to form a sturdy foundation for the squad's stunts.

Bases. The base is, as the name indicates, the foundation of any stunt. A base is the bottom person in the mount, the foundation upon which a stunt is built. It's important for the base to be strong and steady. Strong shoulders and arms are a must, as are strong legs that enable the base to remain still and controlled at all times. Many people think it's the flyers and the tumblers who need all the balance, but bases need balance, too. A base

Flyers need to be lightweight and agile in order to be tossed into the air for stunts. They must exert control over their arms and legs as they move.

who loses that sense of balance finds the whole stunt tumbling down around her.

Flyers. Sometimes called mounters, flyers tend to be the smallest members of any squad, simply because they're the lightest, and therefore the easiest to lift and catch. Body control is crucial, and a flyer must know where those arms and legs are at all times. Whether being tossed in the air or mounting a base to strike a pose in a pyramid display, a flyer needs to be agile and aware. When the flyer climbs to the top of a pyramid, the judges want to see performance and poise, not someone who looks like they're struggling to climb a mountain.

Spotters. The importance of spotters can't be overstated. Because cheerleading routines can be dangerous when they incorporate challenging pyramids or tosses, spotters become absolutely necessary. It is a spotter's main responsibility to make sure that, in the event of an accident, the flyer's head does not hit the ground. Beyond this responsibility, the spotter needs to know every aspect of the squad's routine. When the spotter knows the routine, she knows where the dangerous points in the routine are, and can redouble her efforts to help insure the safety of everyone on the squad. Back spotters have particular responsibilities, too. They are the primary catchers of the flyers, so back spotters need to be strong, confident, and able to handle fast-moving weight.

Tumblers. Tumblers add style and flash to a competitive squad's routine. It's one thing for a squad to strike a visually interesting pyramid for the judges. It's something else for that pyramid to be held in place while tumblers

A tumbler, at far right, adds flash to the action of the University of Kentucky varsity squad, while spotters stand below each pyramid or toss, ready to help catch the flyers and make sure they are protected in case of an accident.

are performing cartwheels and handsprings. It's important for tumblers to look energetic and crisp in their tumbling, not slow and methodical. If you've been taking gymnastics classes for a few years or more and you like cartwheels, walkovers, and handsprings, the role of tumbler may be just for you.

Captain. Not every team has a captain, and no specific physical skills are necessary to be a captain. Even so, if your competition team has a captain, you should understand how important a job it can be. The captain (or co-captains, since many teams have more than one captain) is expected to set the pace for the rest of the team. A captain needs to have a strong work ethic, an ability to get along with everyone on the team (even the team members who may not always be so nice), and a sense of responsibility. The captain should get along with the coach and be able to express concerns to the coach that any team members might have. That's especially important when some team members aren't comfortable speaking directly to the coach themselves. In many ways, the captain serves as an inspiration and a role model for everyone on the team.

The Competitive Landscape

There's a lot of cheerleading happening out there. In 2001, according to *Time* magazine,

> Some 40 groups organized regional and national competitions, most of them between December and April. "Competitive cheer" has become the fastest-growing high school sport for girls; about a third of U.S. high schools have competitive teams, sometimes in addition to more traditional spirit squads.

> "Today, more than three million girls and guys across the U.S. make up school, all-star, recreation, and youth

The University of Kentucky's varsity cheerleading squad has won the UCA's National College Cheerleading Championship 12 times: in 1985, 1987, 1988, 1992, 1995, 1996, 1997, 1998, 1999, 2000, 2001, and 2002.

WHAT ARE THE JUDGES LOOKING FOR?

Each competition will have its own specific score sheet that the competition judges use to rate each squad. Generally, teams are scored on a maximum of 100 points. Typically, judges will be ranking competition squads on the following:

Jumps and stunts: How well does the squad perform overall cheerleading skills?

Spirit: How appealing to the crowd is the squad, and how well does the squad utilize showmanship and project its personality?

Difficulty: How difficult are the stunts that the squad is performing, and do they require squad members to utilize a wider range of skills?

Choreography: Are the squad's movements crisp and synchronized, and are the transitions from stunt to stunt smooth?

Overall effectiveness: Is the squad incorporating all of the required elements of the competition, and is there a clear level of creativity and energy evident in the team's presentation?

Some cheerleading competitions have all judges evaluating all squads in all categories, while other competitions have judges who pay attention only to specific things. For example, at some competitions, there is a penalties judge who makes sure that squads don't use illegal stunts, step out of bounds on the performance floor, or use more than their allotted time.

In all cases, the best thing to do is to get a copy of the competition's judging form as soon as possible so that you and your squad can focus on doing the best you can under that competition's specific rules and regulations.

league teams," *American Cheerleader* magazine reported in 2002. "There are more than 50 cheerleading camp and competition companies and more all-star teams than anyone can keep track of. . . . Today, girls and guys in more than 50 countries on six continents take part in the sport."

In June 2002, *USA Today* quoted one expert as counting no less than 72 national or regional competitions for college, high school, or youth teams. With so many competitions to choose from, how does anybody try to make sense of it all?

The good news about cheerleading's crowded and confusing competition calendar is that wherever you are, and at whatever skill level your squad might be, and whatever style of cheerleading your squad prefers, there's a competition just for you.

To gain an understanding of what the competition options are for your geographic area, and for your squad's skill level, attend a few county or state competitions. Go to a summer cheerleading camp.

The biggest national competition is held by the National Cheerleaders Association (NCA). The NCA College National Championship, held in Daytona Beach, Florida, and Dallas, Texas, is televised by CBS Sports. In 2002 the grand prize winner of the NCA College Nationals was the University of Central Oklahoma. The NCA also holds competitions for junior high, high school, and all-star teams. Cheer Athletics won the senior division of the NCA All-Star Nationals in 2002.

The second biggest national competition is the one held by the Universal Cheerleaders Association (UCA) in

To earn high marks, a cheerleading squad must have crowd appeal and lots of spirit.

Orlando, Florida. The UCA has three distinct competitions, one each for college, high school, and all-star teams. They are all televised on ESPN.

In 2002 the University of Kentucky won the UCA's National College Cheerleading Championship for NCAA Division 1-A schools. The University of Kentucky squad has won UCA's National College Cheerleading Championship an unprecedented 12 times.

Tennessee's Craigmont High School took first place in the varsity large co-ed division at the 2002 UCA High School Nationals, while Kentucky's Greenup County High School placed first in the large varsity competition. The 2002 UCA National All-Star large varsity competition was won by the Memphis Elite All-Stars.

The UCA also sponsors the Six Flags Series, a variety of cheerleading and dance team competitions that take

THE FIRST WORLD CHEERLEADING CHAMPIONSHIP

For two days in May 2000, Warner Brothers Movie World outside of Dusseldorf, Germany, was the center of the cheerleading world for the first World Cheerleading Championship.

The competition, held by the National Cheerleaders Association (NCA) based in Dallas, Texas, saw 12 countries participating for awards in six divisions. Participating nations included the United States, Germany, Chile, Great Britain, Austria, Slovenia, Italy, Spain, Finland, Switzerland, Sweden, and Denmark.

The United States, represented by Club Cheer of Dallas, took the World Cheerleading Championship title. Santiago's Chile Cheer took second place, and the Braunshweig Wildcats from Braunshweig, Germany, came in third. Only two-tenths of a point separated the three teams as they headed into the finals.

"It was an unbelievable honor to be asked by the NCA to represent the United States at this event," said Club Cheer coach Brandi Noble with tears in her eyes. "This is definitely the beginning of something extraordinary, something very big."

Jumps and stunts, as well as overall difficulty, are some of the things judges look for in competition.

place at Six Flags amusement parks across the United States.

In addition to the NCA and the UCA, *American Cheerleader* lists no less than 36 national competitions. Among the many groups who organize cheerleading competitions are the United States Cheerleading Association, the American Cheerleaders Association, and the American Spirit Championships. There's also the World Spirit Federation, the Worldwide Spirit Association, and the World Cheerleading Association. The list of sponsors and competitions goes on and on.

Each organization hosting a national competition has its own divisions and categories within which teams compete. Some competitions emphasize advanced dance or stunts, while others feature novice teams. Entry fees can range from a few dollars to nearly $100 per person, but the costs of competing can be much higher if there is travel involved to get to the competition.

Rules and safety guidelines govern each type of cheerleading competition. It is important to know the specifics of these rules before you start training, because often there will be descriptions of what can and can't be done in routines. Here are a few examples of the kinds of rules and regulations you might see:

- No jewelry is permitted during performances. This includes bracelets, necklaces, earrings, and belly button rings.
- Each team must bring at least two copies of its music to the competition on cassette tape or compact disc.
- The time limit for each routine is two minutes and 30 seconds. Timing starts at the first obvious movement or sound, and ends when the end of the routine is obvious to the judges.
- Flipping dismounts exceeding one rotation are prohibited.
- Cheating of any kind will not be tolerated.

Each competition has its own system of awards. At some competitions, every participating team gets a

The University of Kentucky's 2002 varsity cheerleading squad poses for a group photo. They are the only team to have won back-to-back national championships three separate times.

trophy, while at others, only the top teams get awards. Sometimes clothing, medals, and gift certificates are awarded. At the NCA National Championships, for example, winners receive banners, jackets, gift certificates, and trophies.

Within each competition, of course, there are multiple divisions in which squads compete. For example, the Cheerleaders of America (COA) 2002 Nationals saw nine divisions of competition, such as junior varsity, senior all-star, and power divisions. Within each of these divisions there are specialized categories of competition. The varsity division of the COA 2002 Nationals featured competitions for small non-mount squads, large and super-large non-mount squads, small mount squads, medium mount squads, large and super mount squads, co-ed squads, and large co-ed squads.

Beyond the national competitions, there are countless competitions on the regional, state, and local levels. Like the many national competitions, each has its own rules regarding entry fees, specific rules and regulations for performances, the awards that are presented, and the types of squads that are welcomed into the competition.

Epilogue

ome day, when you are a veteran cheerleader, you may look back at how nervous you were the first time you prepared for a competition. Back then, you felt like you were sweating bullets. You may remember every tiny detail of the day, from the color of the gym walls to the hairstyles on the judges to the cracks on the floor on the way to the performance mats.

When you first started out, you wanted to be on the cheerleading squad so badly. You knew there would be a lot of work involved, but you had no idea exactly how much work you would be doing. It didn't always feel like work, though. Sometimes it felt like play, even with all

The thrill of winning is one of the many experiences squad members can share. Celebrating a good performance at the AmeriCheer Nationals, these cheerleaders show their excitement.

the practices and the coach's orders and doing the same moves over and over and over and over again, just to get them exactly, precisely right. It may sound like a lot of work to someone who doesn't do it, but it was also a lot of fun to be practicing so intensely with your fellow squad members.

Those first few months on the squad were difficult, but you stuck with it, until you looked forward to each new competition with enthusiasm and a sense of adventure. You welcomed the work, because you knew it would lead

CREATE A "RULEBOOK" FOR YOUR SQUAD

One way to help build unity on a cheerleading squad is to have a set of rules that everyone understands and follows. Some of the rules can be serious, some of them can be silly. Here are a few suggestions for very specific rules you and your fellow cheerleaders might want to include.

- All cheerleaders must maintain a C+ average or better in their academic studies.
- No cheerleader may miss more than two practices in any calendar month.
- Cheerleaders should not wear their uniforms unless participating in official squad activities.

Talk it over with your coach and the other cheerleaders. If everybody can agree on and stick to a clear set of rules, and if those rules can be enforced consistently, then everybody will benefit. There will be fewer misunderstandings and arguments, and everyone will have a lot more fun.

Competing can be a wonderful experience and chance for a squad to gain both poise and confidence.

to another opportunity to prove to the judges how good your squad is. You knew it was also another opportunity to prove to yourself and your team that you could do the job, and do it well. Even if you lost you knew you had tried your hardest.

During your first few months on the squad you felt like your attention was spread out all over the place. There were rules and regulations to learn and be aware of, cheers and routines to practice, schedules to follow,

Making friends and memories and gaining confidence in yourself can be even more important than winning.

fundraising to worry about, and so much more. Sometimes it all seemed overwhelming. But you helped lead the squad's fundraising efforts, and it was one of their best years ever. You didn't miss a single practice, and you learned to juggle your homework and your cheerleading practices. Everything became easier as you got used to the work.

Looking back, you may recall your first competition, when you almost dreaded seeing your parents and your friends in the stands. You worried that they might call out your name for everyone to hear.

Once you've gained competition experience, you will be able to practice and perform with confidence in front of any audience anywhere. Preparation for the competitions may also bring your family closer together as they support you in your goals.

GRADE YOURSELF

Part of being a cheerleader means having to take a close look at yourself. Do you have a tendency to argue a lot? That's something that could hurt you as a cheerleader.

Here are a few statements to say out loud about yourself. For each statement, grade yourself with one of the following: "strongly agree," "generally agree," "generally disagree," or "strongly disagree."

- I get along well with others.
- I am attentive in class.
- I have a good attendance record.
- My general appearance sets a positive example for my school.
- I get good grades.
- My classmates look at me as someone who is willing to be helpful.
- My teachers have nice things to say about me.

There are no passing or failing grades in this quiz, but if you answered "strongly disagree," to three or more statements, then you probably have a little work to do.

Nobody expects cheerleaders to be perfect, of course, and you should never pressure yourself to be perfect. However, as a cheerleader, you should understand that you serve as a role model. That means that other people are looking up to you as an example of positive behavior.

As a member of your cheerleading squad, you have developed a whole new circle of friends. Your squad practices together, laughs together, cries together, travels together, competes together, and wins or loses together. You share experiences with one another that you think about in the late hours as you are trying to get to sleep. When you do so, you find yourself falling asleep with a smile on your face. Having such good friends and teammates to share so many special times with is like a dream come true.

It's amazing to you that coming to another competition can get all these kinds of thoughts working in your head. You will look at yourself in the mirror as you check your uniform, and feel like you've traveled a million miles to get there.

You know you still have miles to go. You're not at the end of the journey, you're at the beginning. This isn't the first competition you've been in, and it won't be the last. You welcome the challenge, and you are comfortable meeting the challenge.

You may have never thought you could feel so comfortable with all the pressures of a competition. Cheerleading can teach you how to handle all kinds of pressures big and small.

The more you compete, the more relaxed you'll be. It will be work, but fun at the same time. The excitement of the competition will never diminish.

At every competition, you will take your place on the performance surface with poise and confidence, feeling good about your team and the routine you're all about to perform. More than anything, though, you will feel a kind of confidence about yourself that you've never felt before doing anything else. Deep down, you know it's the kind of self-confidence that will stick with you for the rest of your life.

Glossary

arch – A position in which the back is curved.

back spotter – A spotter who is the primary catcher of a flyer.

base – The bottom person in a stunt who remains in contact with the floor. The base supports the mounter in a stunt.

chant – A short, repetitive yell performed continually throughout a game (example: "De-fense! De-fense!"), or a short routine with words sometimes involving the crowd.

cheer – A longer, more spirited yell that is performed only during official breaks of a game. Often, a cheer will utilize a variety of motions and stunts.

dismount – The act of safely returning to a floor position following a stunt.

flyer – The person who is elevated into the air by bases to perform a mount. The flyer can also be called a mounter.

handspring – A spring from a standing position to the hands, and back to a standing position.

jump – A spring into the air in which both feet leave the ground and the body assumes a given position.

mid-base – A base who is not in contact with the cheering surface.

mount – Often used interchangeably with "stunt," a mount is any skill in which one or more persons are supported in the air.

mounter – Another term for a flyer.

pyramid – A stunt involving one or more flyers supported by one or more bases and linked together.

routine – A choreographed sequence of moves.

split – A position in which the legs are spread apart in alignment or sideways one in front of the other

spotter – A person who is in direct contact with the floor and may help control the building of, or dismounting from, a mount. This person may not provide primary support for the mount, meaning that the mount or pyramid would remain stable without the spotter. The primary responsibility of the spotter is to watch for safety hazards. The spotter is positioned on the floor in such a way as to prevent injuries, with particular concern to the head, neck, and back areas.

straddle – A position where the legs are straight out and apart.

stunt – Any maneuver that includes tumbling, mounting, a pyramid, or a toss.

toss – A throwing motion by the base or bases to increase the height of the top person in the mount, during which the top person has no contact at all with the base or bases.

transition – A choreographed maneuver that enables a team to move from one highlighted stunt to the next.

tumbling – Gymnastic skills used in cheerleading.

Internet Resources

http://cheerleading.about.com/index.htm
> An About.com directory of hundreds of Web sites, categorized by subject matters like Cheerleading 101, Cheers and Chants, and Fundraising.

http://www.americancheerleader.com
> The official Web site of *American Cheerleader* magazine features message boards, chat, and a wide variety of articles available to subscribers.

http://www.cheerhome.com
> Created in 1999 "for the benefit of cheerleaders and cheerleading coaches," CheerHome.com features news, message boards, articles, and resources for learning more about cheerleading camps, competitions, and college programs.

http://www.cheerleading.net
> Cheerleading.net has links to hundreds of Web sites for cheerleaders and coaches at all levels.

http://www.cheerleading.org.uk
> The Web site of the British Cheerleading Association has information about championships, camps, and clinics in the United Kingdom.

http://www.nationalspirit.com
> The National Spirit Group is the parent company of the National Cheerleaders Association, organized in 1948 by Lawrence Herkimer.

http://www.varsity.com
> Varsity.com offers information on cheerleading and dance. The Universal Cheerleaders Association (UCA), a leader in cheerleading safety and stunt innovation, is also part of Varsity.com. The UCA is one of the largest cheerleading camp providers and competition sponsors in the world.

Further Reading

Chappell, Linda Rae. *Coaching Cheerleading Successfully.* Champaign, Illinois: Human Kinetics, 1997.

French, Stephanie Breaux. *The Cheerleading Book.* Chicago, Illinois: Contemporary Books, 1995.

Kuch, K.D. *The Cheerleaders Almanac.* New York: Random House, 1996.

McElroy, James T. *We've Got Spirit: The Life and Times of America's Greatest Cheerleading Team.* New York: Berkley Books, 1999.

Neil, Randy, and Elaine Hart. *The Official Cheerleader's Handbook.* New York: Fireside Books, 1986.

Rusconi, Ellen. *Cheerleading.* Danbury, Connecticut: Children's Press, 2001.

Scott, Kieran. *Ultimate Cheerleading.* New York: Scholastic, Inc., 1998.

Index

CRAIG PETERS has been writing about various aspects of sports and popular culture for more than two decades. His daughter, Alexandra, began her dance and cheerleading training when she was two years old. By the age of 13, Alexandra had competed on several school and recreation teams and been named captain of her middle school cheerleading squad. Craig has long ago given up the idea that this might be a passing fad for his daughter.